RIGHTS AND RESPONSIBILITIES

USING YOUR FREEDOM

Frances Shuker-Haines

A Blackbirch Graphics Book

RSVP

RAINTREE STECK-VAUGHN

PUBLISHERS

Austin, Texas

320.4
(1)

A Blackbirch Graphics Book

Printed and bound in Mexico

1 2 3 4 5 6 7 8 9 0   RRD   98 97 96 95 94 93

Library of Congress Cataloging-in-Publication Data

Shuker-Haines, Frances
        Rights and responsibilities: using your freedom / Frances Shuker-Haines
        p.   cm.— (Good citizenship library)
        Includes bibliographical references and index.
        Summary: Examines the rights and responsibilities of being a citizen, discussing such topics as free speech, interest groups, voting, taxes, jury duty, and running for office.
        ISBN 0-8114-7355-4   ISBN 0-8114-5583-1 (softcover)
        1. Civics—Juvenile literature. 2. United States—Politics and government—Juvenile literature. [1. Civics. 2. Citizenship.] I. Title
II. Series.
JK1759.S57   1993
320.473—dc20   92-25732
                                                                        CIP
                                                                         AC

Acknowledgments and Photo Credits

Cover: ©Dru Nadler; p. 4: ©Bob Daemmrich; pp. 7, 10: The Library of Congress; pp. 9, 15: AP/Wide World Photos; pp. 12, 17, 25, 38, 42, 43, 45: ©Dru Nadler; p. 18: Gamma/Liaison; p. 20: ©Chaisson/Gamma-Liaison; p. 26: ©Jim Bourg/Gamma-Liaison; p. 29: ©Diana Walker/Gamma-Liaison; p. 33: ©Bill Swersey/Gamma-Liaison; p. 35: © Stuart Rabinowitz; p. 36: ©Rhia/Gamma-Liaison.
Graph by Sandra Burr.

Photo research by Grace How

4/2/94

Contents

On Being a

Citizen

"Government of the people, by the people, and for the people."
—*Abraham Lincoln*

"Ask not what your country can do for you—ask what you can do for your country."
—*John F. Kennedy*

"We hold these Truths to be self-evident, that all Men are created equal, that they are endowed by their Creator with certain unalienable Rights, that among these are Life, Liberty, and the Pursuit of Happiness—That to secure these Rights, Governments are instituted among Men, deriving their just Powers from the Consent of the Governed."
—*The Declaration of Independence*

Opposite:
Many American citizens are proud and patriotic.

"We the People of the United States, in Order to form a more perfect Union, establish Justice, insure domestic Tranquility, provide for the common defence, promote the general Welfare, and secure the Blessings of Liberty to ourselves and our Posterity, do ordain and establish this Constitution for the United States of America."
—*The United States Constitution*

"We live in a democracy, which is precious, especially to those of us who have come from countries without freedom. If the public expects to have a role in voting and the decision-making of government, they need to better understand the world around them. If not, democracy is just a public-relations exercise and isn't worth anything."
—*A recent Russian immigrant*

Many voices, one subject: democracy. America has always been a country of many voices. From the African American whose great-great-grandfather was a slave, to the Vietnamese who just immigrated, to the Bostonian whose ancestors were on the Mayflower. From our country's Founders to the president to the baby born last night in your local hospital. All of these people are Americans, and all of these people have something very important in common: citizenship in a democracy.

Thomas Jefferson wrote the Declaration of Independence, one of our country's most important founding documents.

The United States is a democracy that was started in a revolution. But our country also started a revolution in the way people were governed. That revolution is still being felt today, as countries in

7

Eastern Europe and all over the world strive to become, like us, governments "of the people, by the people, and for the people."

What does that mean? It means our leaders are elected by the people they lead. It means that our laws are supposed to serve *our* needs, not the whims of a dictator or king. It means that "we the people" decide the laws of the land. But a democracy can reflect the wishes of the people only if the people express those wishes. We are not only allowed, not only encouraged, but also duty-bound to take part. It's never too early to become involved in politics—be it in your school, community, state, or even the White House. If you start now, it's a habit you'll find hard to break.

Playing a Part in Our System

What gives us the right to be involved in our democracy? Citizenship. If you were born here, you've got it. If you are an immigrant who has been naturalized, you've got it. It means you must obey the laws of the land. But it also means that you may try to change those laws if you think they are unfair.

One of the most effective ways to change laws is by voting. But not everyone has the right to vote. Children under 18 can't vote, nor can convicted criminals or the insane. Before 1866, people who had been slaves could not vote. And before 1920, women could not vote. Before 1971, in some states, people under 21 could not vote.

★ ★ ★ ★ ★ MADD Enough to Make a Difference ★ ★ ★ ★ ★

Candy Lightner turned a tragedy into a crusade that has saved lives, changed laws, and opened the eyes of thousands of Americans.

In 1980, Candy's daughter was killed by a drunk driver. On the day of her daughter's funeral, Candy started MADD, or Mothers Against Drunk Driving. Its goal: to put an end to drunk driving once and for all.

MADD is a citizen-action success story. It has changed laws and changed minds. Since it began, every state has toughened its drunk-driving laws and raised its drinking age to 21. Sober, "designated drivers," who drive for others who have been drinking, have become common. Hosts now usher intoxicated guests into cabs or the cars of friends instead of into the driver's seat.

How did Candy do it? By visiting her state governor's office every day until he would listen to her. By talking to the press to get her cause known. By talking to senators and representatives in Washington. By giving speeches all over the country to educate people about her cause. Candy did what every citizen is entitled to do: organize, speak out, and contact elected officials. As Candy herself has said: "I do feel that if you believe in something badly enough, you can make a difference."

Candy Lightner is the founder of MADD.

And yet, even without the vote, which is the all-important "tool" of democracy, African Americans and women were able to change the laws about voting just by speaking out, forming groups, and making their cause known. Abolitionists were partly responsible for ending the practice of slavery in this country. Both black and white abolitionists traveled and spoke and made their cause known. Eventually, their dream came to pass—slaves were freed and given the right to vote. "Suffragists," as we now call them, were women who fought for the vote in the early part of this century. In the end they convinced enough people that women in America, too, should be allowed to vote. The Nineteenth Amendment, which gave women the vote, was added to the Constitution in 1920.

Abolitionists and suffragists are just two of the many kinds of people who have worked to fight injustice, to right wrongs, and to keep America at its best. The history of this country is filled with people who took chances, stood up for what they believed was right, and worked for change. We not only allow our citizens to act on their beliefs, we strongly encourage them to. Freedom of belief is our right as citizens. It is our duty to keep the government working for us as citizens. And the only way to do that is by being informed, aware, responsible in your community, and concerned about politics. And remember, you're never too young to start.

Opposite:
John Brown was a famous abolitionist who was imprisoned, convicted on a charge of treason, and hanged.

11

Getting

Involved

Before you can become involved, you have to become informed. The only way to form an opinion, target a problem, or seek out a solution, is by knowing the facts. That isn't as hard to do as it sounds. Television, newspapers, magazines, pamphlets, position papers, interest groups—these are all excellent sources of information that are easy to find and easy to use.

The Right to Free Speech

The First Amendment to the U.S. Constitution guarantees freedom of speech. That means people in this country can think and say whatever they want, even if someone else doesn't like it. It also

Opposite:
All American citizens are guaranteed the right to free speech and are encouraged to use that right to get involved in important issues.

13

means newspapers (and other forms of news media) are free to print whatever they feel the public should know. The truth is never a simple thing to define. But newspapers try to print the truth as they see it, even if that "truth" is unpopular, or makes some important people look bad. This freedom of the press is crucial to democracy. It means that the government can't hide its actions from the people. It means that we have the right and the opportunity to know what's going on in our country—whether we like it or not.

Sometimes people complain about the media. They think reporters "go too far." They think newspapers are too critical and report only the bad news. These complaints may be valid. But imagine the alternative. Without a free press and our basic right to know, how would we find out what was *really* going on in the world?

Here's an example. What if your town's water supply was being polluted by a local chemical company? Wouldn't you want to know about it? You'd need the facts in order to decide what you could do about it. But would you get those facts? You couldn't necessarily count on the chemical company to tell you, especially if they were doing something wrong. But a newspaper would have no reason not to tell you how and why the company was contaminating the water. And because our press is free to publish whatever it wants, that newspaper would have every legal right to tell you.

Sometimes the biggest changes come about because one person sticks to his or her beliefs about what's right and what's wrong.

Rosa Parks was a black Montgomery, Alabama, seamstress. Like all blacks, she was required by law to sit in the back of the bus she rode to and from work every day. One day she just refused. She knew segregation was wrong. She knew racism was wrong. Her small act of defiance got her arrested and fined. But it also gave birth to a bus boycott and the entire civil rights movement of the 1950s and 1960s. Rosa Parks is a heroine because she did the right thing according to her conscience, in the face of laws that were wrong.

There have been others, and there will be more. There will always be people who change the world not by running for office or going to law school. They do it just by believing in something and sticking by that belief. Let them inspire you to do the same.

Rosa Parks helped to spark the civil rights movement of the 1960s by standing up for what she believed.

Now think about what it would be like if the government controlled the press (as it does in some other countries). The government could then choose to tell us only what it wanted us to hear. But what if it was doing things we didn't approve of? How could we effectively protest or support the government's actions if we didn't know what those actions were? Our votes wouldn't count for much if we didn't know what, exactly, we were voting for.

Newspapers, magazines, and news programs, keep us informed. They help us to see many sides of each of our society's problems and allow us to make up our own minds about the issues of the day.

Stories That Made a Difference

There are many examples of stories that the press has told that have made a difference in government policy and in our lives. *Silent Spring*, by Rachel Carson, was originally published in a magazine called *The New Yorker*. It was the first article (it later became a book) to talk about the dangers of using pesticides. A pesticide called DDT was later banned, in part because of this article.

The New Yorker also published John Hersey's book *Hiroshima*, which told of the devastating effects of the atomic bomb on that Japanese city. Had it not been published, millions of Americans might never have known the stirring details of the first use of an atomic weapon.

Opposite:
One of the best ways to stay informed is to read newspapers and magazines on a regular basis.

Good television news programs can offer a great deal of information to viewers in a short period of time.

The *Washington Post* reported on the Watergate scandal during the administration of President Richard M. Nixon. Without that reporting, we might never have known that our president had broken the law.

If you want to stay informed, you've got to read and listen. The best place to start is the newspaper. You can read a big-city daily like *The New York Times*, or your local paper. (To get the most out of reading newspapers, it helps to know your way around them—see page 24.)

Television News

Newspapers, because of their size, can cover more stories more thoroughly than the television news. But if you don't have a lot of time, the TV news will fill you in. There are several different kinds of news programs to choose among: the local news, the network news (which covers both the national and international news), "magazine" news shows (such as *60 Minutes* and *20/20*), and news analysis programs (such as the popular *MacNeil/Lehrer News Hour* and *Nightline*), which deal in depth with one or two of the day's top stories.

News Magazines

News magazines, such as *Time, Newsweek,* and *U.S. News and World Report* have fewer stories than a daily paper, but they have the space for a more thorough discussion of the week's events. They also report on social trends, the arts, and science.

Interest Groups

Another source of good information is interest groups. There are organizations devoted to just about *everything*. Ask your school or local librarian for help in locating directories of organizations. And then contact that group for the information you want or need.

As for politics, before you can decide which politicians to endorse in any given election, it's important to find out what they stand for. Contact

their campaign headquarters for pamphlets and position papers. Try attending rallies or debates. Listen to the candidates' speeches. Ask questions if you can. What's important is what the candidates believe, what they've shown they are committed to, what they've done, and what they plan to do in the future. What's *not* important is how they look on television, how slick their ads appear, or what kind of clothes they wear. Would you rather be led by a pretty face or represented by someone with brains, determination, and ideas that he or she can put into use to make the neighborhood, state, country, or world a better place?

Getting the Facts

The more informed you are, the better you'll be able to judge a politician who is running for office or evaluate a proposed plan or law. The more informed you are, the better you'll be able to form your own opinions about the people representing you and the issues that matter the most to you. You'll start assembling your own set of values—and that's something that's uniquely yours, something that helps to define who you are. You may not be completely liberal or straight-down-the-line conservative, a committed Democrat or a devoted Republican. That doesn't matter. What matters is that you care, that you think about the world around you, and that you believe in important ideas. That makes you a good citizen.

Opposite:
Many citizens are active in interest groups that promote a special cause, such as saving the environment.

Think About Issues That Matter to You

You can get started any number of ways. Think about the things that matter to you the most. Then look around and see what you can do to make a difference in your own community. Are you particularly concerned about the environment? Look for a recycling program that needs volunteers to help sort bottles and cans. Worried about the homeless? Help out at a soup kitchen, or organize a clothing drive. Do you think education is important? Then you should think about your school. Are there changes you'd like to see there? If so, you should think about joining the student government. Or consider circulating a petition about unfair school policies, so the administration knows how the students feel. Or think about joining forces with other kids to clean up the playground and paint a mural. These kinds of local activities can be especially satisfying. You can see the results right away. You can feel the effect you're having right where you live.

However, you needn't limit yourself only to neighborhood activism. If politics is your interest, you can volunteer for the campaign of a candidate for any kind of office, from the state legislature to Congress, from city council to the presidency. You might start out by licking envelopes or handing out flyers, but you'll be *involved*, and that's what really counts. Think about other ways to help a particular campaign—could you help get people registered to vote? Help shut-ins get to the polls on election day? It doesn't matter if the tasks are less than glamorous—you'll know you're helping make democracy work.

Even though you're too young to vote, your government representatives still represent you. In many ways they are *your* representatives. You have every right to register your opinion with them. Pick up a pen and write. You'll find most government addresses and phone numbers in the blue pages of your phone book. Or send your views to your House or Senate representative, mayor, governor, or president. Here are some addresses and phone numbers for your representatives in Washington:

> For the House of Representatives:
>   (The name of your representative)
>   United States House of Representatives
>   Washington, DC 20510
>   (202) 224-3121

> For the Senate:
>   (The name of your senator)
>   United States Senate
>   Washington, DC 20510
>   (202) 224-3121

> For the U.S. president:
>   (The name of the president)
>   1600 Pennsylvania Avenue
>   Washington, DC 20500
>   (202) 456-1414

So you want to stay on top of things. You go out and buy the newspaper, but don't know where to begin. Some tips:

• For a brief overview of the events of the day, most papers have a **news summary** or **index** to consult.

• The most **important stories**, plus the **national** and **international news**, usually appear on the front page and "run over" onto other pages inside the first section.

• **Local news** is often in the second section of the paper.

• Newspapers also include a forum for opinions on the **editorial pages** (usually located near the end of the first section). They include editorials, columns, guest editorials, and letters to the editor. Reading the editorial pages can help you to clarify your thinking. By reflecting on other people's opinions, you might start to form some of your own.

• An **editorial** expresses the newspaper's view on a particular issue or news item. It might be an endorsement of a candidate in an upcoming election, or thoughts about a new bill to fight crime. A **guest editorial** is an editorial by a writer for another newspaper, an expert on some topic, or other invited contributor.

• **Columns** are regular pieces in which their authors, called columnists, offer their opinions on a range of subjects. Some columnists are humorists. Others specialize in bringing to light the experiences of certain groups of people. Some are just "roving" commentators who like to pick a different issue each time and explore it in their own way.

• **Letters to the editor** provide an opportunity for readers of the newspaper to express their opinions on current events and issues of interest. They also allow the paper to become a community forum for discussion and debate.

• The people who write the newspaper articles are called **reporters** or **journalists**. Journalists have a duty to be objective. That means they are supposed to report only the facts of a story, without allowing their opinions or feelings to affect their writing. That way, the reader can make up her or his own mind about the issues.

Once you know and care about what's happening around you, you're ready to become involved. There are many levels of involvement possible, from schoolroom to town hall, from congressional campaign to the White House itself.

Finding the information you want in a newspaper takes a little practice and some knowledge of how the newspaper is organized.

At Long Last:

Adulthood

Your life doesn't change on your 18th birthday, but your legal status does. In almost every state, you legally become an adult on that day, with all the rights and responsibilities that go with it. Some adult privileges may already be yours, such as the right to get a driver's license, to work without a permit, and to get married with or without the consent of your parents. But, by and large, you can call yourself a full, legal adult from the age of 18 on!

Becoming a Voter

One of the most important things that happens when you turn 18 is that you get the right to vote. Now, after years of caring about politics, being

Opposite:
The first step in becoming a voter is to register in your hometown area.

involved in your community, and staying on top of the news, you can finally affect the government directly, through voting.

The right to vote is something people all over the world, including the founders of this country, have given their lives for. It's important that we not take it for granted. And it's very important that we exercise it every time we get a chance.

Voter Registration

Even though you are eligible to vote at 18, however, you cannot simply show up at your polling place on Election Day and cast your ballot. You must *register* to vote first. Unfortunately, many people find this process too difficult, overly time-consuming, or threatening in some way, and they don't do it. And obviously, if people are not registered, they are not going to vote. Don't let that happen to you! Registering to vote is not hard; you just have to do a little simple detective work to find out how.

Where you register varies from state to state, so it's up to you to find out where to go. Who might know: the League of Women Voters, a research librarian in your city, town, or school, your local Democratic or Republican party office, a politician's campaign office, the county clerk's office, your local election board, not to mention your social studies teacher, or your mom and dad. Most of the time, you can register at your local town or city hall.

Once you've registered to vote, you are allowed to vote in all elections, big and small, local and national. It's crucial that you do so. How can we have a government that represents the people, if the people aren't willing to take the time to make themselves heard?

National conventions are a colorful and exciting part of a national election.

Too Many Non-Voters

Non-voters are a big problem in our country. In the 1988 presidential election, only 50.2 percent of the eligible voters voted. In congressional elections, the numbers are even lower. Compare these low numbers to those from other democracies in the world. In Australia, 95 percent of the people who can vote do; in Italy, that number is 93 percent; in Japan, 73 percent. Why aren't we voting?

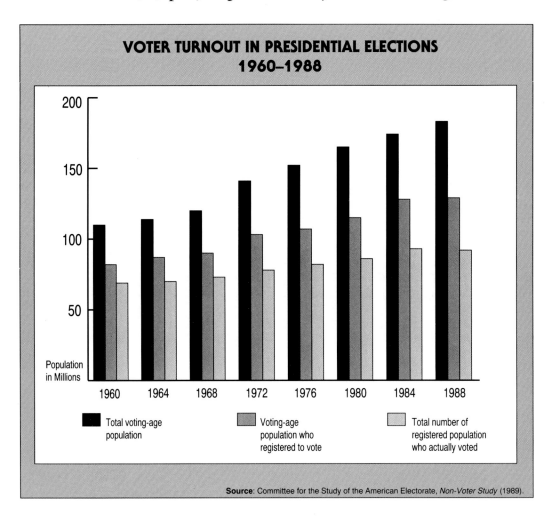

VOTER TURNOUT IN PRESIDENTIAL ELECTIONS 1960–1988

Source: Committee for the Study of the American Electorate, *Non-Voter Study* (1989).

Young people are less likely to vote than older ones; having more education makes you more likely to vote; the more money you have the more likely it is that you'll make it to the polls on Election Day. But as low as voter turnout is, think about this: 70 percent, or a majority, of all *registered* voters voted in the 1988 election. Clearly, then, the greatest single obstacle to voting is non-registration.

In fact, registering for the vote *is* more difficult in this country than in many other countries. The procedures for registration in America vary from state to state. The place to go to register changes depending on where you live. How far in advance of the election you must register to vote also changes from state to state.

Voter Turnout in the Past

There are historical reasons for some of these voting obstacles. In the 18th century, some politicians used to try to win elections fraudulently, by hiring people to vote for them over and over again. As a result, some states adopted tough registration laws, to ensure that each eligible person voted only once.

Another reason for roundabout registration procedures was racism. After blacks were granted the constitutional right to vote, some southern states got around that right by making it extremely difficult for blacks to register. These southern states developed literacy tests that would be impossible for anyone, black or white, to pass. Or they imposed "poll taxes" that would be impossible for poor people, many of whom were black, to pay. While these practices were later declared illegal, some of the more subtle obstacles remain on the books, making it harder for all of us to participate in our government as much as we should.

So don't be discouraged. Find out how to register *before* you turn 18, and do it as soon as you can. Those who are 18 to 21 years old are the group with the *lowest* voter turnout. You can be part of changing that.

In some states, you will be asked to declare a party affiliation when you register. You do not have to choose a party. But keep in mind that in many parts of the country, you cannot vote in primary elections unless you are a member of a political party. This is because political parties use primary elections to choose their candidates from among their own ranks.

Old Enough to Serve

Opposite:
Once an American citizen is 18 years old, he or she is eligible to serve in the armed forces.

Voting is a right and a responsibility. Another responsibility that you acquire when you turn 18 is registering for the draft. Every male citizen must go to the post office and register when he turns 18. This means that if the United States enters a war and decides to institute a draft (because it needs more soldiers than our volunteer armed forces can supply), it will have the names of all the young men in the country "on file."

There's more to adult responsibility than just obeying the law and pulling a lever on Election Day. Being a member of a community of people brings with it many responsibilities.

One responsibility you have to yourself and to others has to do with alcohol. You owe it to yourself not to abuse alcohol. It can ruin your body, destroy your brain, and even kill you. If a drinking problem turns into alcoholism, it can wreck the lives of those around you and break the hearts of those who love you. And you owe it to everyone out on the road *never, ever* to drink and drive.

Another area of responsibility is drugs. Before you use them, you might, again, want to think about their effect on the community as a whole. Do you want to risk lives by your own reckless behavior (by driving under the influence, for example)? Do you want to support an "industry" that is largely responsible for the alarming rise in violence in our country? Do you think breaking the law is an example of good citizenship?

And while sex is an extremely private subject, there are public aspects of it, too. Part of being a responsible adult in this day and age is to be responsible about sex. Sexually transmitted diseases are on the rise, and the worst one of all is, of course, AIDS. Don't contribute to the spread of AIDS! Don't sleep around. If you won't "wait till marriage," at least get to know your partner well before having sexual relations with him or her and always use a condom. This may seem like a strange aspect of being a good citizen, but it's all part of caring about your community, and being committed to the public good.

Registering for the draft is *not* the same as being drafted. When the draft begins, not every young man will have to serve. There are always exceptions —health problems and deep moral or religious convictions against war are two of the reasons that young men are not called to fight.

When adult rights and privileges are abused, the lives and safety of an entire community are put at risk.

Minors and Adults

Legal adulthood means many more things, too. But like so many regulations in this country the laws regarding adulthood vary from state to state.

However, the difference between being an adult and being a minor remains relatively constant. A

minor cannot enter into legal contracts. A minor cannot be sued for breaking a contract. A minor does not face the same judicial system when he or she commits a crime. That is because children aren't considered responsible for breaking the law in the same way adults are. For one thing, children can't always understand the consequences of their actions. Very young children might not always know the difference between right and wrong. And we believe that children deserve to be rehabilitated; that, in most cases, there's still a chance of teaching them how to be productive members of society in the future.

The Juvenile Courts

All states have some sort of juvenile court system. Unlike regular courts, the cases in these courts are tried in front of a judge who specializes in juvenile law, rather than in front of a jury. The judge decides on sentencing, but he or she does not send children to jail. Reform school, special programs, and professional counseling are some of the alternatives.

There are exceptions. Older children (usually over 14) who have committed particularly horrible crimes, such as rape or murder, can be tried and sentenced as adults in most states.

But once you're 18, you are an adult in the eyes of the law. And you will bear the responsibility of being tried and punished as an adult if you decide to break the law.

Opposite:
In the American legal system, juveniles have different rights from adults and are treated in a separate system of justice.

The Grown-up's Guide to

Being a Great Citizen

Being a citizen means being a member of society. It means caring about and involving yourself in the political process of the country. It also means caring about and involving yourself in helping your own community, or even just your block. A society that is founded on the idea that every person counts falls apart if every citizen doesn't do her or his part.

So part of being grown-up means being an individual with opinions, beliefs, values, and stands on the issues. Part of it is caring about the whole group, and the individuals who make it up.

Opposite:
Being a citizen of the world means taking action for the causes you believe in.

Counting Our Citizens

One time that your individual contribution will make a difference in the "group" of the United

States of America is when the census comes around every decade.

All households in the United States are supposed to respond to the U.S. census every 10 years. The census is a questionnaire put out by the government to get an idea of who make up the country and what they're like. The census helps answer: How many people live in the average house or apartment these days? Which cities have the most people? Which parts of the country are growing most in population? Which are shrinking? How many single-parent households are there? These are some of the many things the census hopes to find out.

Each decade, census-takers do the best they can to get *everyone* in the country to respond. They organize a mass mailing that is supposed to go to every home address in the country. New housing, residences in business districts, and other addresses often don't make the lists. They print up posters and set up hot lines in 10 languages. They even travel into subway tunnels and bus-stop waiting rooms to try to count the homeless. Why all the bother? It's important that the census-takers get responses from as many people as possible, since government funds are often given (or not given) to cities, counties, and other local divisions according to the number of people the census says live there. If a lot of people don't respond in a certain city, for example, that city could lose a lot of government money in the following 10 years.

Congressional districts, too, are established or changed on the basis of the census. If a particular area has shrunk in population, it might lose a representative in Congress. Or, if a city's population has swollen significantly, it might qualify for an additional representative.

As citizens, we can help the census along by responding honestly and quickly. Let's not make the census-takers' job any harder than it is!

Another thing that adults (usually) do is make money. Money, of course, is extremely useful in life, and most people don't have a lot to spare. But many people find a way to contribute to charities and causes anyway. This is another way to stay involved, to see a direct connection between your contribution and changes in the world around you.

Becoming a Taxpayer

Speaking of money, as soon as you start making it, you will have to start paying taxes—another responsibility of the adult citizen. Taxes may often elicit a groan from the adults around you, but in fact they are really one of the most important contributions we make to the government. They are the funds our government uses to pay for our social programs, to keep our country rolling, driving, flying, armed, and productive. Without taxes, we would not have Social Security to support the elderly and disabled, welfare to support the poor, schools to educate our youth. Paying taxes is

Paying taxes is one of the most important contributions a citizen can make to government.

another way we participate in the government. However painful it is on payday, we all have a responsibility to support our country in this way.

But we also have a right to care where our tax money is going. That is why it's so important to be thoughtful when you pick political candidates for any office—because they'll be spending your money. You have a right and a responsibility to influence how they do that.

Serving on a Jury

Another way that you will be asked to serve your country is through jury duty. That is because citizens are guaranteed the right to a trial before a jury of their peers. The way the government rounds up those "peers" is through jury duty. If you are a citizen, you receive a notice in the mail, and then report to the appropriate court when asked. However, you may or may not find yourself on a jury. If you are picked to serve, it will then be your duty as a citizen to remain as impartial as possible, and make the fairest decision that you can make.

Serving Others in the Future

While jury duty is mandatory, being a volunteer is also a way to serve others. As an adult, your time, experience, and expertise are all very valuable. Using your skills to tutor others, being a Big Brother or Big Sister, volunteering to do job counseling at the

Taking action in your community is one way to play a part in your local government.

43

community center, answering the phones at a fund-raiser, getting your company to match funds for employees' charitable contributions—these are just a few things you will be able to do as an involved adult citizen.

Running for Office

Once you're an adult, you can also get involved in government in the most direct way possible: running for office. The basics of how to do that varies from county to county and from state to state. You'll have to be at least 25 years old to run for Congress, 30 to try for a Senate seat, and 35 to run for president. Every politician was a kid once, and then became an adult who cared enough to try to make things happen. Don't assume that only "other people" can govern; anyone can. That's one of the best things about a democracy.

Being a Citizen of the World

Being a citizen isn't just confined to your street, your town, your state, or even your country. Now, more than ever, we are also citizens of the world. Because of overpopulation, mismanagement of natural resources, pollution, and carelessness, our entire planet is under siege. The environment is becoming increasingly fragile, and we all need to do what we can to preserve it. These might be our most important duties as citizens: to reduce, reuse, and recycle. We can help preserve our planet so we

may all live to see better governments and better times. The simple acts of picking up trash, taking your newspapers to be recycled, and walking to the store instead of driving may seem tiny, but they can add up to a big difference. One person acting in the best interests of all the people—that's the essence of good citizenship, and the hallmark of a responsible and productive adult.

Participating in school politics can be a good first step toward building a life of political involvement.

45

Glossary

abolitionists   People who fought to abolish slavery in the 1800s.
activism   Getting politically involved.
census   Process of counting the citizens of a country, usually done
    every ten years.
convictions   Deeply held beliefs.
draft   Process by which the government calls upon its citizens to serve
    in the military.
felons   Criminals who have committed serious crimes.
journalist   Person who writes objective, factual stories for publication.
mandatory   Required.
minor   Person under the age of 18.
naturalization   Process by which immigrants and illegal aliens may
    become American citizens.
peers   Fellow citizens; colleagues; people of similar backgrounds.
segregation   Forced separation of people by race.
suffragists   Women who fought for voting rights in the late 1800s and
    early 1900s.
tutoring   Teaching others.

For Further Reading

Bradley, John. *Human Rights*. New York: Franklin Watts, 1987.

Fagan, Margaret. *The Fight Against Homelessness*. New York: Franklin
    Watts, 1990.

Hirsch, Charles. *Taxation: Paying for Our Government*. Austin, Texas:
    Raintree Steck-Vaughn, 1993.

Kronenwetter, Michael. *Politics and the Press*. New York: Franklin
    Watts, 1987.

Newton, David. *Taking a Stand Against Environmental Pollution*. New
    York: Franklin Watts, 1990.

Scher, Linda. *The Vote: Making Your Voice Heard*. Austin, Texas:
    Raintree Steck-Vaughn, 1993.

Schlesinger, Arthur M., ed. *The Peace Corps*. Broomall, Pennsylvania:
    Chelsea House, 1990.

Index